WHAT DO THEY DO?

POLICEMEN and FIREMEN

by **CARLA GREENE**

pictures by **LEONARD KESSLER**

An **I CAN READ** Book

HARPER & ROW, PUBLISHERS   New York, Evanston, and London

To Terry, Wendy, and Craig,

who love to read

WHAT DO THEY DO?
Policemen and Firemen
Text Copyright © 1962 by Carla Greene
Pictures Copyright © 1962 by Leonard Kessler
Printed in the United States of America

Harper & Row, Publishers, Incorporated,
49 East 33rd Street, New York 16, N.Y.

Library of Congress catalog card number: 62–8036

WHAT DO THEY DO?

I CAN READ
ABOUT POLICEMEN

badge

whistle

handcuffs

stick

police station

motorcycle

ticket

helicopter

pilot

I CAN READ
ABOUT FIREMEN

helmet

gas mask

smoke

pump truck

hose

hook-and-ladder truck

rescue

firehouse

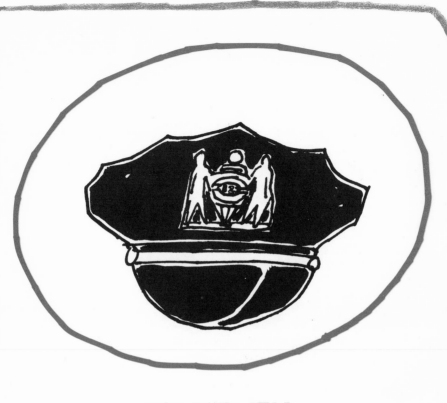

POLICEMEN

Here is our friend, the policeman.

He is tall. He is brave.

He helps to keep us safe.

The policeman has a badge

on his cap.

He has a badge on his coat.

He has a gun.

He has a whistle.

He has handcuffs.

Sometimes he carries a stick.

This policeman walks and walks.

Up this street. Down that street.

The streets he walks

are called his beat.

He watches everything.

13

Sometimes the policeman needs help
on his beat.

He calls the police station.

More policemen come to help him.

14

Here is a traffic policeman.

He stands in the street.

He stands there

in summer and winter,

in rain or snow.

So many cars!

Some go this way.

Some go that way.

How can we cross the street?

The traffic policeman

blows his whistle.

He puts up his hand.

The cars stop.

Now we can walk across the street.

Whizz-zz-zz! ZZ—zz—zz!

Here is another

traffic policeman.

There he goes on a motorcycle.

Stop that car!

It is not safe to drive so fast.

The driver is breaking the law.

"Pull over," says the policeman.

He takes out

a paper and pencil.

He gives the driver a ticket

for speeding.

The driver will have to pay a fine.

Whir—rr! Whirr—rr!

There go two more

traffic policemen!

They ride in a helicopter.

One policeman is the pilot.

The other policeman

watches the road.

He sees an accident.

The accident blocks the road.

Cars cannot move.

The policeman calls for help.

Soon the road is clear.

The cars can move again.

Policemen in helicopters

watch for many things.

They watch for fires.

They watch people swimming.

Sometimes they look for someone

who is lost.

The policemen help to save him.

Calling all cars!

Calling all cars!

An accident at Green and Tenth.

Someone is hurt.

Ee—ee—ooo! Ee-ee-ooo!

Make way for the police car.

All cars stop!

Let the police car pass.

The police car must hurry!

Policemen learn to give

first aid.

A policeman can help

someone who is hurt.

A policeman knows what to do

before the doctor comes.

Calling all cars!

Calling all cars!

There is a burglar

at 27 Park Street.

26

Ee—ee—ooo! Ee—ee—ooo!

Flash! There goes the police car.

Hurry, hurry, hurry!

The policemen must catch

the burglar.

Policemen are trained

to help keep us safe.

A policeman learns to run fast.

He learns to jump high.

A policeman learns to wrestle.

A policeman learns to shoot.

But he does not shoot

unless he must.

A policeman does not want

to hurt anyone.

29

Help! Help!

A man fell into the river.

Here comes the police boat.

The policemen will save the man.

A parade! A parade!

Everyone wants to see the parade.

No pushing! No pushing!

The parade must have

room to pass.

31

Here comes a policeman

on a horse.

Is he part of the parade?

No.

He is a mounted policeman.

The policeman and his horse

keep the people back.

In some towns motorcycle policemen

do this job.

33

A little boy has lost his way.

"I will help you

find your father,"

says the policeman.

34

It is best not to get lost,

of course.

But if you do get lost

in a big park

or at the beach,

tell the first policeman you see.

He will help you.

The policeman will help you

any time, any place.

He is your good friend.

He is a good friend to all.

FIREMEN

Here is our friend, the fireman.

He is strong. He is brave.

He helps to keep us safe.

The fireman wears a helmet.

There is a badge on his helmet.

On the badge is the number

of his fire company.

The fireman wears a rubber coat

and rubber boots

to keep him dry.

Sometimes he wears a gas mask

to keep out smoke.

40

41

Clang! Clang! Clang!

The fire bell rings.

Zeep! Zoop!

The firemen slide down the pole.

Get on the fire trucks!

Get set to go!

Ee—ee—ooo! Ee—ee—ooo!

Off goes the Fire Chief

in his red car.

Ee—ee—ooo! Ee—ee—ooo!

Clear the way! Clear the way!

Here come the fire trucks!

45

There goes the pump truck!

Hang on, firemen!

Into your coats!

On with your helmets!

Hang on!

Ee—ee—ooo! Ee—ee—ooo!

Make way for the pump truck.

What big hoses!

Ooo! Ooo! Ee—ee—ooo!

Watch out for the long

hook-and-ladder truck!

A fireman steers at the front.

Another fireman steers at the back.

Hang on, firemen!

Soon the firemen reach the fire.

Quick, quick, quick!

They hook up the hoses.

The pump truck pumps the water.

Swish, swoosh, swoosh!

Big streams of water

shoot out of the fat hoses.

The firemen can spray

plenty of water on the fire.

Up goes the tall ladder

on the hook-and-ladder truck!

Up the ladder go

two firemen.

Now they can reach the top

of the building with their hose.

50

"Help! Help! Save me!" calls a lady.

A fireman goes up a ladder.

Quick! Hurry, hurry!

The fireman helps the lady down.

"Thank you! Thank you!"

says the lady to the fireman.

The fireman is happy.

It is a fireman's job

to save people from fires.

"Help! Help!"

The man is too high up.

The ladders cannot reach him.

Out comes the big net!

"Jump, jump!" the firemen call.

The man jumps into the net.

See him bounce!

53

The man is safe.

But he is hurt a little.

Here comes the rescue truck.

The firemen on this truck

are called the rescue crew.

They are trained

to give first aid.

They will help the hurt man.

Part of the fire is out.

But the river side

of the building is still burning!

Toot! Toot! Toot!

Ee—ee—ooo! Ee—ee—ooo!

Here comes the fire boat

with more firemen on it.

The firemen turn their hoses

on the fire.

They spray high! They spray low!

The fire is still burning.

Firemen, firemen, put it out!

Spray more water

with your big fat hoses!

58

At last, the fire is out.

But there is more to do.

The firemen pump out the smoke.

They mop up the water.

They sweep up the ashes.

They make sure that

the fire is really out.

The firemen go back

to the firehouse.

Some scrub the hoses.

Some clean the fire trucks.

Everything must be made ready

for the next fire.

Matches
Start
FIRES...

ED HOPPER
FIRE CHIEF

These firemen are on night duty.

They go to bed

at the firehouse.

They leave their pants

in their boots

at the side of the bed.

61

Clang! Clang! Clang!

Another fire!

Quick! Quick! The firemen jump

into their pants and boots.

They pull on their shirts.

Zeep! Zoop!

Down the pole!

Onto the fire trucks.

Get set to go!

Ee—ee—ooo! Ee—ee—ooo!

Watch out for the fire trucks!

The firemen are on their way

to put out another fire!

By day and by night,

firemen help to keep us safe.

The fireman is your good friend.

He is a good friend to all.